Catch That Star!

'Catch That Star!'
An original concept by Jenny Jinks
© Jenny Jinks 2022

Illustrated by Monica Garofalo

Published by MAVERICK ARTS PUBLISHING LTD
Suite 1, Hillreed House, 54 Queen Street,
Horsham, West Sussex, RH13 5AD
© Maverick Arts Publishing Limited May 2022
+44 (0)1403 256941

A CIP catalogue record for this book is available at the British Library.

ISBN 978-1-84886-878-6
Printed in India

www.maverickbooks.co.uk

This book is rated as: Yellow Band (Guided Reading)
It follows the requirements for Phase 3 phonics.
Most words are decodable, and any non-decodable words are familiar, supported by the context and/or represented in the artwork.

Catch That Star!

By Jenny Jinks

Illustrated by Monica Garofalo

Jem and Jack are looking up.

They see a star zooming down.

They see a light high on the hill.

"Catch that star!"

"That is not a star," Jack tells Jem.

They see a light in the town.

"Catch that star!"

"That is not a star," Jem tells Jack.

They see a light near the water.

"Catch that star!"

"That is not a star," Jack tells Jem.

They see a light in the big oak.

"Catch that star!"

The light zips up and down.

Quick! Get a net.

"We got the star!"
yell Jack and Jem.

But it is not a star.

"Let's let it go," sighs Jem.

The bug zooms up.
Lots of bugs join it.

Jem and Jack look up.

"It is a star!" Jem tells Jack.

Quiz

1. Jem and Jack are looking…
a) down
b) around
c) up

2. What do they see zooming down?
a) A net
b) A star
c) A rocket

3. Who else was out camping?
a) Dogs
b) Rabbits
c) Bats

4. What does Jack get?
a) A box
b) A net
c) A bucket

5. What makes the star at the end of the story?
a) Bugs
b) Flowers
c) Nets

Turn over for answers

Book Bands for Guided Reading

The Institute of Education book banding system is a scale of colours that reflects the various levels of reading difficulty. The bands are assigned by taking into account the content, the language style, the layout and phonics. Word, phrase and sentence level work is also taken into consideration.

Maverick Early Readers are a bright, attractive range of books covering the pink to white bands. All of these books have been book banded for guided reading to the industry standard and edited by a leading educational consultant.

To view the whole Maverick Readers scheme, visit our website at www.maverickearlyreaders.com

Or scan the QR code above to view our scheme instantly!

Quiz Answers: 1c, 2b, 3a, 4b, 5a